Denise Ostuni Fucito was born and raised in East Northport, LI, NY. She raised her children in Kings Park, NY and in 2007, moved all year round to her summer home on Candlewood Lake in New Fairfield, CT.

In addition to being a mother, Denise has held a wide array of roles, including a legal secretary, public relations professional, business teacher, self-employed corporate trainer/coach/keynote speaker, career transition counselor, director of a trade/business private school, and human resource executive. She holds a Bachelor's Degree in Business Management from New York Institute of Technology and a Master's Degree in Education from Dowling College.

During the pandemic, Denise became motivated to tap into her expansive experiences and began writing of lessons learned in her personal and professional life. She is following her motto by George Eliot: "It's never too late to be what you might have been."

This memoir is lovingly dedicated to my mom and dad, Jenny & Tommy Ostuni, whose encouragement and support guided me through my maiden voyage of writing. They provided ample material and I am forever grateful for their presence in my life. And Mom, you were a good sport.

I could not have continued writing these entries without the encouragement of my family and friends. The feedback kept me going and made me want to continue to lighten our spirits during such troubled and scary times.

I am eternally grateful for my children: Gina, her husband Mike (Shanahan), my precious grandchildren, Tommy and

Scarlett, my sons Andrew and Jamie and my nephew Patrick. You all keep me grounded, sane and proud. Hopefully this journal will serve as a manual that will guide you when I enter my 80s.

Thank you to my siblings: my brother Johnny, my brother Charlie (and his wife Lori) and my sister Angela (and her husband John Larson). You've always been a source of support and understanding and we are so fortunate to maintain a family bond that is unbreakable. You were all very much a part of this journey, even though you were absolutely no help physically!

Also, thanks to my Caruso Cousins – Cathy, Terri, Anthony, Troy, and Janine. We are the luckiest group of adults that have the privilege of still celebrating milestones with our crazy parents. Thanks Uncle Vinnie, Aunt Patty, Uncle Andy and Aunt Eva for continually providing insights into my parents' traits. When all of us gather and go 'down memory lane' we are fortunate to simultaneously create new memories. Can't wait until the next reunion.

Thank you to my friends Tina Newman, John Krueger, Kim Falci, and Virginia Russell – you have each served as my 'help' desk support person at various times throughout my life and I am so lucky to be able to count on you as sounding boards and dear friends.

To my 'Summa Sistas' – Barbara Lynch, Cathy Marasco, Donna DeSantis, Gloria Craven, Jean Kavanagh, Judy Garbowski, Karly Becker, Kathy Shanahan, Katie

Cyganowski, Maria Stonecipher, Maureen Clegg, Maureen Roberts, Nancy Hyland, Maura Rail, Theresa Stark, and Teresa Wohr, as well as their husbands, and my pals Jules Leo and Scott Stevens. A special thanks for providing me with daily friendship and comfort. I appreciate you all for keeping my social calendar full all year round and for preventing me from ever having to refer to my life as lonely or dull. You inspire me when I am with you individually and when we are together as a mob. May we never be too old to party all night – even if we have to social distance.

And finally, thanks to the Austin Macauley publishing team, especially my production coordinator, Hannah Scott, for guiding me in my maiden writing voyage and making sure I didn't sink like the Titanic.

Denise Ostuni Fucito

55 Days and Counting

My Quarantine Adventure With Mom And Dad

AUSTIN MACAULEY PUBLISHERS™

LONDON • CAMBRIDGE • NEW YORK • SHARJAH

Ordering Information
Quantity sales: Special discounts are available on quantity purchases by corporations, associations, and others. For details, contact the publisher at the address below.

Publisher's Cataloging-in-Publication data
Fucito, Denise Ostuni
55 Days and Counting

ISBN 9781649794208 (Paperback)
ISBN 9781649794215 (ePub e-book)

Library of Congress Control Number: 2021918935

www.austinmacauley.com/us

First Published 2021
Austin Macauley Publishers LLC
40 Wall Street, 33rd Floor, Suite 3302
New York, NY 10005
USA

mail-usa@austinmacauley.com
+1 (646) 5125767

Introduction

In February 2020, I was working in Manhattan as VP of Human Resources for a private finance company. In an effort to cut my Connecticut to NYC commuting time, I rode the NJ Path Train twice a week to stay with my son in Jersey City. During this time, there was so much confusion regarding the onset of Covid-19. In mid-February, I was ill for three days and clueless as to whether I had a virus, flu, or was just feeling under the weather. I later discovered that I had several symptoms that are common with Covid, but I was never tested, and so I can't say whether I had the virus or not.

My annual vacation to Florida was planned for March 8th through March 23rd. When I landed at Tampa International Airport, I rented a car and headed to my friend's house near Venice for two days. These were the early stages of the pandemic. On March 10th, I hopped in my convertible and drove from the West Coast to my parents' condo on the East Coast. They live on North Hutchinson Island, a small section that lies on the beach between Fort Pierce and Vero Beach. By the time I reached them, some social distancing was in place, and we were all fist-bumping each other. My last day in a restaurant was at breakfast after church with a group of their friends on Sunday, March 15th. Then the isolation began, no more gatherings, no more activities, just stay-at-home fun in their 1600 square foot condo on the ninth floor. My 16-day vacation morphed into 55 days of 'bonding' time.

While hanging with my parents, both 83 years old and married for 62 years, it dawned on me that our time in isolation would be filled with insanity. I started writing a diary and sending my daily entry to over 70 family members and friends.

By the time we returned home to Connecticut, I was unemployed, we were virus-free, and miraculously we were still speaking to each other.

In Connecticut, we live next store to each other, so I am still 'counting' our time together as an ongoing adventure. And, of course, I am so grateful that I am able to do so.

Tuesday – March 17th, 2020
Dear Diary

This coronavirus debacle has been life-altering.

What I thought would be a joyful two-week vacation in sunny Florida with my parents has instead become an indefinite stay that is no longer vacation but rather a prison sentence.

I am surrounded by retired people who never know what day it is. There is no distinction between a weekday or a weekend. Hard to fathom, but I am slowly turning into that person who has no clue what day or date it is. I'm beginning to wake up feeling like Bill Murray in the movie Ground Hog's Day; same weather, same scenery, the same everything.

I spend my mornings working at my computer, praying our company doesn't fold, putting me out on the streets without a job. Of course, I can't pray in the church because they are "closed." Never in my lifetime did I think that I would be banned from my house of worship.

When I'm not working, I spend my downtime taking a walk on the beach, swimming in the pool, and reading on the balcony. Nothing wrong with that, right? Hmmm.

- We eat at 4:30; my stomach has yet to adjust to this new schedule.
- Mom and I fight in the kitchen all day long; who's the better cook? who makes the most mess? On and on, their Florida kitchen is definitely not big enough for the two of us.
- Before we went into full quarantine, we had several 'domino' nights with Aunt Patty and Uncle Vinnie. The longest game ever and Dad always wins while Mom takes way too long to make her move. They really should have created this game with the highest tile being a 10 instead of 15.
- The TV is always blasting, even with a closed caption on 24/7. I seriously might lose my hearing because of it.
- They bicker over the ridiculous stuff, and I'm used to that because their marriage has always been solid and they rarely go to bed mad. However, being privy to their silly squabbling has me murmuring, *"shoot me now,"* a hundred times a day.

I miss my kids and my precious grandson. Thank God for Facetime. Gina and Mike are doing fine in New Fairfield; Andrew will be heading there soon (from Jersey City), and he'll work from my house. Jamie is busy working, and when he calls, I get a good laugh at his police stories. Yesterday he broke up a fight over toilet paper at the local mall for real, seriously. He told the group of maniacs, *"Would you like me to throw a roll of TP in the aisle and sit back and watch you all tackle it?"* They took offense to his comment.

I've been told by my siblings, "*Good Luck*" and to keep Mom and Dad under full quarantine (which involves drugging Dad). They say, "Come home now," then "stay put," then "drive home now." At this point, I will just have to determine when the time is right to leave. I am truly grateful that I am here spending this quality time with them. I'm no fool to think that my friends wouldn't be thrilled to be given more time with their parents, so I embrace this responsibility, and I will wake up every morning wondering if anything new will happen and if I can withstand another game of dominoes.

Please let this crisis pass without harming my family, friends, and colleagues.

And please give me the strength to get through it and *keep my sanity*.

Yours truly,
Denise

Thursday – March 19th, 2020
Dear Diary

When Life Hands You Lemons, Forget the Lemonade Get a New Life!

That's a chapter from the book I'm writing (and living at the moment).

'Do You Laugh or Cry? A Guide for the Downsized'

So, I got laid off a few hours after my last diary entry on Tuesday.

It's always shocking even we expect it's coming.

I will survive.

It will be a challenge to reinvent myself at 61, but I've always preached, "*It's ever too late to be what you might've been,*" so who knows what the future holds.

I will survive.

I'll tighten my budget, let my hair go gray, paint my own toenails, lose some weight naturally (my new food budget will supply me with a diet of carrot sticks that should do the trick), and I'll apply all sorts of other cost-saving measures.

I will survive.

I still don't have access to my house of worship, but saying my rosary on the balcony in the warm sunshine is a good substitute.

Speaking of balcony, I haven't flung myself off the ninth floor yet, which means hanging with Mom and Dad has been OK so far.

I took Mom to the doctor yesterday. She has gout. I printed a list of things she can and cannot eat and realized that in the last three days, she pretty much ate everything on the 'don't eat' list, *hence the flare-up*.

Their latest squabble was a doozy. Dad said, "*I'll do the laundry, Dollie (his nickname for her). Don't worry about it.*" Of course, she pulled a Jenny and began sorting the laundry and putting it into two piles on the floor by the washer. God forbid she waits for him to follow through. Needless to say, I mumbled, "*Shoot me now,*" about five times while that battle went on.

It's been a while now, so tonight we will play dominoes again. Uncle Vinnie said, "*See you at 4:30,*" and all I can think was, *damn, my stomach has actually adjusted to this early eating, and I better go prepare dinner asap.*

Later,

Denise

Saturday – March 21st, 2020
Dear Diary

When we played dominoes the other night, I prefaced the game with "*Be warned that anything you say or do can wind up in my diary entry.*" They responded to me with a threat that if me, my siblings, and my cousins continue to make fun of them, we will be taken out of their wills. Needless to say, I can't afford that right now, so I was a good girl the rest of the night.

As part of our Ground Hog's Day routine, Dad gets up early and reads the paper, then goes for a walk. Mom reads the paper and begins her daily routine of insanity. Then I get my coffee and read the paper and complete the 'jumble' and 'cryptogram' puzzles. Mom then immediately removes the paper from the premises and sticks it in the outside community recyclable bin. Except for the other day, she pulled another 'Jenny'. While reading the paper, I got up to refill my coffee, and when I turned around, it was gone. Just like that gone! No puzzles, no paper, and me counting to ten before I went off with my sarcastic remark of "*Did you honestly think I could read the paper and do the puzzles in two minutes?*"

There's a saying I used quite often in my training days, "*You train people how to treat you,*" so now she asks every morning, "*Are you done with the paper?*" It takes 28 days to make a new habit, but I simply do not have the patience to wait that long, so I am using an accelerated method of training.

I hope my friends and family are surviving these challenging times, and like my cousin, Cathy says, "*May your toilet paper roll always be full.*"

Yours truly,
Denise

Monday – March 23rd, 2020
Dear Diary

It's getting tougher now.

I love my siblings. I can't begin to tell you how incredible my brothers and sister are when it comes to supporting me in my good times and bad. The challenges I am now facing beginning week three of 'hanging' with Mom and Dad – more than repay them for their support.

I always enjoyed accompanying my parents on their trips down to Florida in November. We unpack and stock the house and enjoy our new surroundings. I only made a return trip with them once and swore I'd never do it again. Now I remember why.

The term packing has a whole new meaning when it comes to Mom.

Me: "*Mom, you do realize we are not leaving for at least three more weeks.*"

Mom: "*You have no idea how long it takes to do this packing; you cannot procrastinate – so shush and mind your own business.*"

We live out of boxes. If I dare even suggest buying a single food item, I get yelled at, "*We have to get rid of everything we have.*" I feel like I should be on the Food

Network with random food items trying to put together creative recipes. Like what am I supposed to do with a can of kidney beans, one potato, a can of olives, and eggs? Yuk.

Help me, please.

Yours truly,
Denise

Wednesday – March 25th, 2020
Dear Diary

Twelve months a year, my mom has a reversed sleep cycle, meaning she naps all day and then is up all night. It's a vicious cycle and could easily be broken if she would just take some simple advice.

Common sense dictates that she should force herself to stay up all day (no napping allowed) and be tired so she can sleep through the night. This simple solution results in the harsh response, *"Leave me alone, I'm 83. I can do what I want."*

Now, this is a very overused response from Mom. Like when she eats a bag of jelly beans (she's diabetic) or consumes too much pasta and bread (she's celiac), she always responds with her classic *"Leave me alone, I'm 83, blah blah, blah."*

Since logic doesn't work in this household, the only other solution I can think of is to slip some stimulants in her morning coffee, so she stays awake and then some sleeping pills in her evening water. Unfortunately, she takes too many medications (nine pills daily), so I'm afraid I would need a good lawyer if I try this solution.

Yesterday I pulled a Jenny. I took a nap on the balcony at 4:30, went to bed my usual time of 11:00, but woke up at 3:30 am. After reading my kindle, I finally fell back to sleep around 6:00 am. At 7:15, my cell phone buzzed in my ear with the caller ID "Mom Cell," blaring at my eyes. I'm yelling, "*Where the hell are you calling from*?" Now mind you, the guest room I'm in is right outside the kitchen, so she can hear me yelling through the door, not the phone. She slowly responded, "*Oh...*" (long pause), "*I must have butt-dialed you.*"

Instead of being angry, I started cracking up. Why? Because a long time ago, I taught her what a butt dial was, which involved me explaining that you don't have to climb up on the counter and press your butt on the phone, but rather it means an accidental dial.

I'm so proud of her for remembering this lesson. Progress.

No napping for me today.

Later,

Denise

Thursday – March 26th, 2020
Dear Diary

In an interesting reversal of my parents' personalities, I have had the privilege of watching Mom and Dad have the weirdest argument.

Mom, because of her strange sleeping habits, has decided that it is no longer necessary to make her bed in the morning. According to her, she doesn't like the fact that we stay up and she can't, so why should she have to 'unmake' the bed at night by herself? Apparently, this is a burdensome and lonely task.

Now anyone that knows my mother knows she borders as Obsessive-Compulsive about everything. She's organized and orderly, and her label maker is her best friend. But she has suddenly decided that an unmade bed is not the end of the world? Go figure.

Dad's upbringing was much different. He grew up in the "Big House," a nickname for his multi-family home, and it was more relaxed and a little more chaotic. He never even had his own bedroom, so making a bed was not exactly a priority.

After almost 63 years of marriage, it has always been a routine for them to make their bed, either together or by whoever got up last. No exceptions. Ever.

We are going on two weeks of her going on strike and leaving the bed unmade. And every day, Dad has gone in and made the bed because he can't stand seeing it unmade. This morning she comes to me and says, *"Is he a psycho or what?"* I swear my coffee came out of my nose.

I feel like I'm in an episode of the Twilight Zone.

Later,

Denise

Friday – March 27th, 2020
Dear Diary

Yesterday we decided to go on a field trip to Nelson's outdoor produce market. There's nothing like stocking up on fresh fruits and vegetables for the remainder of our stay, especially with all the unhealthy snacking going on. My favorite meme on Facebook: *"I swear my fridge just said: 'What the hell do you want now?"* (Weight Watchers stocks are sure to soar when this is all over).

I gave strict directions that we were to take all precautions, including wet ones wrapped around our hands, and that there was to be no "dilly-dallying," just in and out.

Dad drove like a maniac – speeding and passing people trying to miss the red lights on US1. I'm yelling, *"What on earth is the hurry, we have absolutely nothing else to do, and you are pretending we are in the Indy 500."* Mom is shouting, *"See, this is what I have to put up with, always in a hurry."*

Now at the market, Dad is still in speed mode, quickly putting things in the cart and heading to the checkout. Meanwhile, Mom is slowly wandering about like a "lost child," trying to figure out what else she wants. Dad is already in the car, and I have to go on the line again with

Mom's secondary shopping items. She warns me that when we get back to the condo, we need to beat him inside (send him on a fake errand) so we can put things away slowly. Apparently, when he does it, she can't find anything he puts away.

It's like hanging with the tortoise and the hare.

Needless to say, my head was pounding by the time the day was over. They are so grounded. No more field trips for them for at least a week.

Later,

Denise

Saturday – March 28th, 2020
Dear Diary

How many times were you grounded as a teenager? I was a pretty rebellious one back in the day. One time cousin Cathy and I got caught having a party in the basement when my parents were away. I was grounded the last two weeks of the summer and started to go crazy. Desperate to go to a party I didn't want to miss, I locked the door, popped out the screen of my bedroom window (we lived in a ranch), and escaped, chanting *'freedom at last'* and dancing around like Julie Andrews in the opening scene of the Sound of Music. Then thinking better of it, I realized the serious trouble I'd get in if I followed through with this plan. So I returned to my room, alone again.

Cousin Janine shared a meme on Facebook that stated, "*In an unsettling reversal of my teenage years, I am now yelling at my parents for sneaking out of the house.*" This is so true. When I wake in the morning, and they are nowhere to be found, I panic and run to the balcony to see if their car is still in their parking spot. Did they sneak out and escape? I will ground them if they dare try.

The saying 'You can't teach an old dog new tricks' is a pretty accurate statement. Dad is impossible and will continue to ignore any 'parenting' advice I give. Although I've got Mom trained not to throw out the newspaper prematurely, I still can't get her to relax. She's incapable of it. She's already cleaned out every closet and drawer and packed everything for our return trip. We can't go shopping and she has never, ever watched a tv show or movie without falling asleep in the middle of it. It takes days to erase a saved show on the DVR because, in order for her to finish one, she has to replay it at least five to ten times.

Since I've been here, I have yet to sit in the living room and watch TV with them. It requires patience, of which I have none left. Mom doesn't talk during the commercial; she waits until the show is back on. Questions, comments, you can't even watch the closed caption because she purposely demands your attention. Dad knows how to get around it by asking, "*What would you like to watch, Dollie?*" Then he accommodates her request, knowing she will fall asleep within five minutes, and then he can watch whatever he wants. Me, I just watch the TV in the bedroom, the kitchen, on my laptop or phone. I'm back in my room alone again.

With all this alone time, I am reflecting on comments I've received from several relatives, such as:

"*Wait, it will be your turn soon when your kids are parenting you.*"

And "*Remember, your mom, you shall become.*"

Poor Gina.

Later,

Denise

Sunday – March 29th, 2020
Dear Diary

I just finished attending church (on my laptop), so I'm feeling humbled and spiritual.

Today marks three weeks since I've landed in Florida.

21 days of bliss.

When we are on vacation, we feel like time flies; when we are in isolation, time seems to stand still.

When I was younger, I was a Brownie and then a Girl Scout. I was able to earn some 'badges' with ease, like cooking, camping, music. Others were more challenging, like sewing (ughhh) and bowling (I bowled an 11, and they still gave me the badge). Well, now I think we should create a new badge labeled "30," and everyone gets to earn it for every 30 days they survive isolation with family.

It can apply to everyone, spouses, parents, children; we all deserve a survival badge.

Today I humbly reflect on how great it is to be 'stuck' in Florida cause it's not too shabby.

The pros:

85 degrees and sunny every single day;

The beach is not closed because it is private and beautiful;

Great tan lines;

I haven't blow-dried my hair since I arrived;

No color either, just natural gray coming through the roots;

Nails have returned to their unpolished natural state;

I haven't worn makeup, not once;

Although I brought enough clothes for a month, I've only worn a bathing suit or pajamas. If we go to the stores, I throw a sundress over the bathing suit. When this is all over, I may need a refresher course on how to put on a bra.

And gone is the stress of work, no more HR responsibilities.

Can you imagine my biggest challenge these days is finding the perfect seashell when I go for my daily walk on the beach?

Seriously, this is the task I have assigned myself.

The weather is divine, and being isolated in a 9th-floor condo (#906) with spectacular water views and with your spunky 83-year-old parents could be a lot worse. So, that's all I have to do is hang in there for another week or so, and I'll be on the home stretch and should make it through 30 days.

I'm certain by the end of today, Mom will have given me plenty of stories to tell for the remainder of the week, but for now, I will take a nice stroll on the beach. And when I find that perfect shell, I'm going to turn it into a 'badge' marked 30 and wear it proudly.

God Bless Us All!

Later,

Denise – Troop #906

Monday – March 30th, 2020
Dear Diary

I traveled to Florida with my last canister of Wet Ones. I used them on the plane, the cars, and during grocery store trips. When I first arrived, I told Mom that we have to keep our eyes open for refills because these wet ones are going to become very scarce.

She shouted, "*Don't buy anything, I have a package.*"

When I looked at the package, I commented, *"Ma, these are feminine wipes. You know feminine wipes."*

She looked and replied, "*Oops, I didn't see that, oh well.*"

Then she said, *"No worries, we can use them when we run out of toilet paper."*

Well, the other day, when we left the grocery store, and we were packing the groceries into the back of the van, I reminded her that we need to keep looking for wet ones so we have them for our return car trip. Yes, there were people around as she shouted: "*Don't worry, we have those vagina wipes."*

I almost peed my pants, which, of course, would not have been a problem because, let's face it, I've got vagina wipes.

Classic Jenny.

Later,

Denise

Tuesday – March 31st, 2020
Dear Diary

So yesterday, we had a sibling pow-wow, and it was determined that as long as I can handle it, I should stay put with Mom and Dad here in Florida. No sense in going home to a war zone. They did express sincere concern for my sanity and are appreciative that I'm up for the task.

Now that we have decided we are staying put longer, I convinced Mom that we need to plan at least one full week of meals so we can shop appropriately.

Sunday, she announced that her dinner was going to be a jar of beets. Just beets. I'm like, *"What?"* I realized she grew up on a farm and knew the value of vegetables, but I'm pretty sure beets do not contain protein, nor should they be considered a full meal. Yes, I need to lose weight and should not obsess over food at this time, but I am trying my best to create healthy meals that include several food groups in order to prevent them from counting ice cream as dinner. They do that enough in the summer. *"Oh, we didn't bother with dinner, this is our dinner,"* as they point to a bowl of ice cream.

Mom is determined to eat every food item in the cabinet that she doesn't want to bring home. If I dare mention buying a piece of salmon, she snaps, "*We have to eat what we have,*" and then she opens the freezer, and there is a bag of frozen vegetables, half a loaf of bread, ice cream, and bacon. I know my parents lived through some tough times in their earlier years, but I don't recall them ever having to be on food stamps or eat a jar of beets and call it "dinner."

I went to the stores and bought some salmon which I prepared with sweet potatoes, steamed broccoli, and a fennel salad. I was going to share the meal with just Dad and let Mom chomp on her beets, but in the end, I let her have some too.

In desperate need of restaurants re-opening,

Denise

Wednesday – April 1st, 2020
Dear Diary

When cooking in the kitchen, my mother's OCD really kicks in. She has this obsession that Dad and I should limit our area to one tiny 12 inch square space. *"It's not necessary to use all the countertop." "Every time you two are at the sink, you splash water all over."* OMG, like that's a crime? Really, why bother having a beautiful granite L-shaped countertop if you can't actually use it? I keep waiting for her to say "April Fools," but she's serious.

I consider myself pretty normal when it comes to using my kitchen to its fullest. Spread-out, do your thing, and then when you are finished, you simply take out the spray cleaner bottle, spritz, and wipe it down. If you try to explain this to my mother, *"Spray and wipe. What's the difference how much space you use?"* she will continue to argue that *"it's not necessary to spread out."* Still no April Fools.

It really is just a matter of time before I take to the bottle (alcohol, not spray cleaner). Since I've been here, I have yet to have a stitch of alcohol. Now those of you who know me well know that I love to mix cocktails. I've been dubbed a 'master mixologist' by my friends, and I enjoy my cocktails at all social events. Since I've been in Florida, I haven't bothered since it will just be one more habit I'll have to kick after all this isolation.

Well, that changes today. If you go back and re-read all my diary entries, you would agree that I have a legitimate excuse to drink myself into a stupor. I need to do whatever it takes to earn that "30" day survivor badge.

So, one Dirty Martini is coming right up, but first, I have to go dig in our packed boxes for the jar of olives.

Later,

Denise

Thursday – April 2nd, 2020
Dear Diary

Mom has learned the concept of 'binge-watching' a TV series.

She actually stayed up the other night until 2:00 am watching the Netflix series "Greenleaf."

She started at 4:00 pm and only napped twice her first round.

Mom's very proud of herself for being 'hooked' on this show and is desperately trying to get Dad and me on board.

We have our own addictions to our own shows.

We have zero interest in joining her; knowing she will talk the whole time if we try to watch it with her.

She's behaving like a drunk who doesn't want to drink alone.

As she returned to the couch the other morning to continue her TV marathon, I explained that she has now joined the rest of the world in the art of 'binge' watching.

She looked at me like I had two heads.

"What the heck does 'binge' have to do with it?"
 "It just beats watching the news."

Good answer, Mom. She's right.

Later,

Denise

Friday – April 3rd, 2020
Dear Diary

When I get home, I'll probably need some therapy. The session may go like this:

Me (on the couch): *How do I get my mother to chill out and relax?*

Therapist: *You probably can't.*

Me: *How do I make sure I don't develop the same tendencies?*

Therapist: *You probably can't, and it's probably too late.*

Me: *How do I learn to just deal with her idiosyncrasies?*

Therapist: *There are no tools; you'll have to deal with it the best you can.*

I'm doomed.

Sometimes when the three of us sit down for dinner, the conversations get heated. Instead of biting my tongue, I foolishly lash out about living out of boxes because she insists on packing prematurely. This leads to Mom yelling at Dad and me about how we don't help, blah, blah, blah. The argument then goes off the rails, gets ugly, and ends with her snapping: *"Tough; this is what I do, deal with it."*

The beauty of our family dynamic is that when we have these spats, they just disappear as if they never happened. There is no grudge-holding in this household, and it's a pattern of arguing, fight, move on and be happy. Life is good.

Now I'm trying a little reverse psychology. When Mom gets mad at me and starts making comments about the things I do that drive her crazy, I simply say, *"Just so you know, you're my mother, and you're supposed to love me unconditionally. So, deal with it."*

I think I actually found a way to silence her, and now I don't have to waste my money on therapy.

Feeling sane,

Denise

Saturday – April 4th, 2020
Dear Diary

When the weather gets warmer, you embrace the days getting longer.

When you are in isolation, you definitely want the days to be shorter.

If I get up too early, the day just drags on and on. So I've challenged myself to go to bed as late as possible and then sleep as late as I can, or at least until 9:00 am.

Now under normal circumstances, my mother would be so jealous and so angry that you are able to sleep late; she would make as much noise as possible. My brother Johnny can attest to this action. She'd start banging pots and speak to Dad as if he didn't have his hearing aids in.

But surprisingly, she has been as quiet as a mouse every morning.

Very considerate. And so unlike her.

The other morning, I got up around 9:15 am, I walked out of the room to the kitchen (hair sticking up and only one eye open heading to the coffee machine), and the second Mom saw me, she instantly put her foot on the vacuum cleaner button and started vacuuming. She was probably standing next to it in a ready-to-launch position for an hour, waiting for me to get up.

It's amazing how happy she is when she's cleaning. She pretends she hates it, murmuring all sorts of complaints, but I catch her smiling with joy as she plays "Susie Homemaker."

Now, if I could just find something for Dad to do, I am tempted to go around the condo breaking things just so he can spend a few hours fixing them.

Hmmm, maybe I'll start with breaking the vacuum.

Later,

Denise

Sunday – April 5th, 2020
Dear Diary

I just attended church on my laptop with Mom and Dad, and again I am feeling humble on this completion of four weeks in Florida.

In case you're wondering if I'm making these stories up, let me assure you they are all true. I really thought by now I'd run out of things to write about, but they just keep giving me more material.

I've received many comments from relatives who relate to some of my entries, for example.

Aunt Patty wrote: *"The funny thing about your Diary every day is that anyone who doesn't know Jen and Tommy might think you are exaggerating. As one who has spent years with them, I know every word is the absolute truth."*

So that's one of several testimonials and proof I don't have to make this stuff up.

Last week Mom wrote an email to my siblings saying she wants to get a good defense lawyer to combat my stories, but then she admitted that since it's all true, it would be a 'waist' of time.

When I saw the email, I'm like, *"Ma; it's waste, not the waist."*

Sometimes I just can't help myself.
Give me strength,

Denise

Monday – April 6th, 2020
Dear Diary

Parenting 101

When your children still rely on you for anything: living at home, college, car, insurance, gas, EZ pass, cell phone, you basically own them. You can set rules and force them to do things your way. Once they are truly on their own, you can only guide them and give them advice.

As a mother, this is the first time in my life that my kids are 100% on their own, so I can only sit back and cheer them on or boo them when they make their life decisions. My only hold over them is when they 'visit' my home (and have parties), then I can still set some boundaries.

As a daughter, I am only a visitor in Mom and Dad's Florida condo, and I have to abide by their rules, watch their tv shows, make my bed, etc. Gone is my grown-up freedom. And like the famous line in the movie 'Jaws' when they see the shark up close for the first time: "*You're gonna need a bigger boat.*" Well, we need a bigger kitchen.

They like to use dish rags; I prefer sponges.

They like regular salt and pepper; I prefer granulated shakers.

44

They buy 2% milk; I prefer almond milk.

And on and on

Sharing space is one thing; sharing a kitchen is a whole new beast.

I am trying to wrap my head around the fact that I lived at home with my parents for the first twenty-five years of my life – I didn't go away to college, didn't live on my own in my early 20s. I survived a full twenty-five years of following their rules and respecting their home.

So I ask you, why does it feel like I've been under their roof again for a lifetime? It's only been 30 days.

When we return home to Connecticut (we live next door to each other), trust me, we will be practicing a lot of social distancing for weeks to come.

Later,

Denise

Tuesday – April 7th, 2020
Dear Diary

Mom has this wonderful quirky thing where her shoes and earrings always have to match her outfit. She takes great pride in putting together an outfit with the appropriate accessories for the day.

Well, there hasn't been much going on these days, so now her big field trip is going down to their quaint detached garage. She loves organizing stuff and making crafts. Every once in a while, she chats with neighbors walking by. Because of the social distancing rule (as well as the abundance of hearing aids around here), the chats are very loud. Gossiping is out of the question since everyone can hear your conversation. Nevertheless, she enjoys her daily time outside in the garage.

The other day it was around 12:30 pm, and she left the condo to head to the garage. She returned two minutes later, explaining that before she got on the elevator, she realized her shoes didn't match her outfit, and she wasn't sure if she should bother wearing earrings.

I started cracking up; I'm like, *"Ma, does it really matter?"*

She replied, *"It matters to me."*

Good for her.

Meanwhile, I was still in my pajamas and couldn't even remember if I brushed my teeth yet!

She inspires me.

Denise

Wednesday – April 8th, 2020
Dear Diary

I know everyone can relate to how frustrating it is when you have to play the computer 'help desk' to a senior citizen.

When I was a teacher and a trainer, I loved any lessons on 'soft' skills, career development, marketing, communication, teamwork, etc. But when it comes to 'technical' skills, I have zero patience.

So I conducted a lesson on teaching Mom the difference between AOL and Facebook. When she receives emails on AOL notifying her that one of her 'friends' posted something new on Facebook, she assumes they are sending her a personal email. I've tried every explanation in the book; *"Mom, they are not emails." "You haven't been on your Facebook page in a while, so Facebook, not your friend, is sending you an email, so you'll go check out the posting on Facebook."* She looks at me like I'm crazy, and I have no clue what I'm talking about.

Now being a teacher/trainer, I know the value of kinesthetic lessons. In other words, demonstrate the concept. So I drew a picture of the Facebook logo and put it on one side of the kitchen table, then drew a picture of the AOL logo and put it on the opposite side of the table. I explained they are in the cloud, two different sites floating in the cloud. Then I proceeded to move on to the above explanation about the differences between AOL and Facebook. When I looked up, her face was distorted, and I could tell I lost her in the cloud.

I salute all the teachers trying to teach difficult students and all the parents trying to home school their 'angelic' (so they thought) children. Go make yourselves a nice martini cause it ain't easy.

Later,

Denise

P.S. Appropriate meme on Facebook:

Teachers in 2019: Grossly underappreciated.

Teachers in 2020: Starting to get the respect they deserve.

Teachers in 2021: Crowned as royalty throughout the land, complete with parades and coronations!

Thursday – April 9th, 2020
Dear Diary

The word 'what' has become the most overused word in this condo. All-day long, when the three of us try to communicate from various rooms, that's all you hear is *'what?' 'what?' 'what?'* It is soooooo annoying.

One day Mom asked a question about something that was on TV. Dad was reading his book next to her, and I was in the kitchen. I answered her question (shouting, by the way), and that wasn't good enough. She went on a rampage yelling at Dad why he didn't answer her. Dad explained that I (Denise) answered the question, so he didn't think he needed to respond too. She continued to badger him that he doesn't even answer her, blah, blah, blah. OMG we just need to create a rule that you must face the person you communicate with so we can read lips too.

When we were younger, growing up in East Northport, Mom would have some pretty stressed out days raising the four of us while simultaneously helping Dad run their business.

She had a famous, overused line: *"Go play in traffic on the LIE."* Sometimes she added, *"rush hour"* traffic.

Yeah, we were a little much.

Well, I'm stuck in Florida, far from the Long Island Expressway, and when you are in isolation, you can no longer yell at your kids to go play in traffic or even go out and play, for that matter. Now we are resorted to "go to your room."

Mom keeps trying to ground me. A few times, she has snapped, "*Shut up and get out of here.*" (This mostly occurs when I am trying to explain how to use Facebook.)

So now, when she reprimands me, I just say, *"What? I can't hear you."*

Then I leave the condo to take a walk, which is very safe these days since the roads are traffic-free.

Later,

Denise

Friday – April 10th, 2020
Dear Diary

This morning Mom and Dad successfully snuck out of the condo and went to the stores by themselves.

I got out of the shower and realized I was alone. Running to the balcony, I notice the van was gone. And, of course, they both left their cellphones in the condo.

Now I'm playing detective, trying to figure out where they could have gone. Looking for clues, I search the computer to try and track Mom's 'to do' list (she usually types one daily). No luck. Then I remembered she mentioned she needed basil plants, so I deduce they probably went to Nelson's Farmers' Market.

Now I'm pissed. When I see they have returned, I greet them at the ninth-floor elevator. While stamping my feet with my arms crossed, I yell, *"Gotcha"* when the door opens.

There were neighbors witnessing the exchange, and they began laughing as Mom and Dad looked scared that they were caught. I mostly reprimand them for not taking their cell phones. *"What if something happened?"* *"How can I track where you are if you don't have your phones?"* Then I doled out their punishment. Dad is confined in the office with computer access only. Mom is confined to the kitchen all day (cooking up several meals for the week, with no help from me). I'm going to sit in the living room and command the TV the entire day.

I am starting to doubt my abilities as their babysitter (and I'm secretly hoping my siblings consider relieving me of my duties).

This reverse parenting thing is exhausting.

So I'll be starting my cocktail hour very, very early today.

One Bloody Mary is coming up.

Denise

Saturday – April 11th, 2020
Dear Diary

Dad is still making the bed every day, and it is driving Mom crazier.

She yells to me, "*That f&%$@# made the bed again*!"

He whispers to me, "*Is she a crazy b&%$@#, or what?*"

The other night Mom dragged me to her room to share her new strategy.

She informs me that for the last week, she has unmade only her side of the bed so that when Dad goes to bed, he has to unmake his side.

So now I'm staring at her tucked into her side of the bed and at the other half of an unmade bed with pillows piled high.

I'm thinking to myself; Dad doesn't really think it's that big a deal to throw the stuff on the floor, turn down the covers and climb into bed.

Apparently, she thinks it's a successful strategy.

Well, it can't be that successful because he's still making the bed every day.

Duh!

I refuse to take sides, period.

Me: "*Please, I'm begging you both, do not put me in the middle of this one.*"

I can only mediate so many squabbles. Besides, they don't even think of it as fighting. One minute they're cursing each other, the next minute, *"Dollie, what do you need me to do?" "Honey, can you rub my feet?"*

The other night I was out on the balcony talking on the phone with a friend, and I looked into the living room, and there was Dad sitting up in his recliner watching TV and Mom laying across the couch sleeping, and they were holding hands. I couldn't help but smile and be reminded that it's like living with Dr. Jekyll and Mr. Hyde.

Later,

Denise

Sunday – April 12th, 2020
Dear Diary

Years ago, Mom was invited to dinner with a group of her gal pals in Candlewood Knolls. She volunteered to be the Designated Driver since she never drinks when dining out. The women had a lot of laughs because Mom struggled with all the features on her mini-van, e.g., how to open the side doors, initiating windshield wipers instead of blinkers, etc.

When they were nearing the end of their meal, Mom noticed it was getting dark out and announced to her friends (after they consumed multiple cocktails), *"By the way, I can't drive in the dark."* This resulted in one of the friends ditching her final glass of wine and switching to water so she could take over the Designated Driver responsibility.

This is just one example of many of Mom's *"Duh! What was I thinking?"* moments.

For Easter, I wanted to prepare a nice spiral ham dinner with all the fixings. Mom decided she was craving a rib roast. Her house, her rules. She rifled through her recipe book and began preparations on Saturday to make her rib roast feast. Halfway through her continued meal preparation this morning, she said, *"I don't want to do this,"* and she wandered off to go make flower arrangements.

So I have become the designated driver taking over the completion of our feast. Needless to say, if I should get pulled over, I'll fail the breathalyzer test for sure (hiccup).

Happy Easter!

Denise

Monday – April 13th, 2020
Dear Diary

When you are in extended isolation with the same people, you need to come up with things you can do together and things you can do alone.

On occasion, we each go to our own corner and find a solitary activity. Dad plays spider solitaire on the computer, and I play Rummikub on my laptop. It drives Mom crazy when we find contentment with our own little activity, so she purposely annoys us. When that doesn't work, she'll attempt to watch TV without falling asleep. The woman has the attention span of a gnat.

Tonight I will suggest we play dominoes again. It's been a month since our last game, and we are ready. My cousin Terri once said, *"I think this game is taken way too seriously."* She's right because I don't get as excited about dominoes as our parents do.

Maybe I can turn it into a drinking game. *Hmmm.*

Every time you open the train, you take a sip.

Every time you freeze the game, take a sip.

Every time you score more than 50 points around, take a sip.

Oh, and every time you get that darn double blank tile, you have to guzzle an entire drink.

This should be fun.

Let's hope the night doesn't end with us throwing the tiles at each other.

I'm secretly hoping when I announce to them that I want to play dominoes, my mom will say, *"What? You want to order Domino's pizza tonight?"*

Fingers crossed,

Denise

Tuesday – April 14th, 2020
Dear Diary

Remember when you were a kid, and you had to tell your parents your every move?

"Where are you going? Who will you be with? How are you getting there? Be home before curfew."

In this land of role reversal, I am trapped in; I actually don't have to worry about Mom because she tells me her every move (well, except the one time she 'snuck' out). *"I'm going to get the mail." "I'm going to pick herbs." "I'm going to the garage."*

Dad is a whole different story. When he was in business, he used to drive his secretary crazy because he would just get up and leave the office and never tell anyone where he was going. We used to joke that we should put a bugging device on him so we can track his every move.

Well, here we are 45 years later, and he still just gets up and leaves without a word. We now have the technical ability to put a tracker on a person's cell phone, but the person has to have the phone on them for that to work!

Dad has an old rickety flip phone; he's like a dinosaur.

Texting is not an option. Usually, the phone just sits on his desk all day.

Basically, he lives his life as if the cell phone was never invented.

The only other solution would be to inject him with a chip (like they have for dogs), so we can find him when he is lost.

I am considering teaching him a lesson and trying a little reverse psychology by reverting back to my teenage years.

The lesson involves me stealing the car keys, taking a long drive, and making them pace with worry for hours, wondering where I am. Oh, and I'll be sure to leave my phone on the kitchen counter so they can't contact me.

I am a little hesitant to do this, though, because I might just keep driving and 19 hours later wind up at home in Connecticut.

Later,

Denise

Wednesday – April 15th, 2020
Dear Diary

OK, this vacation has gone on long enough.

When you are in a constant state of Ground Hog's Day, reality begins to allude to you.

This would all be easier if we had an actual end date to this so-called "vacation." How great would it be to start crossing off the days on a calendar leading to our departure date (of our trip from Florida to Connecticut)?

I try fantasizing about the day, years from now, when I can sit around a table and joke about 'that time' I hung with Mom and Dad in Florida for ___ days. But sadly, I can't fill in the blank yet!

Now I can't take all the credit for 'watching over' my parents. I do have a confession to make. Last week I was in the kitchen putting away dishes while Mom and Dad were on the couch watching TV. I inadvertently tripped over a small step stool and landed face down on the ceramic tile floor. Lucky for me, my right palm and my left boob and knee broke the fall, and I was OK after some moaning and groaning. When Mom and Dad ran over to investigate, they looked horrified. Dad stated, *"Good thing you're OK because it's not a great time to have to go to the hospital."*

Mom simply said, "*And you're supposed to be watching us?*" So I do have to admit that we are looking out for each other.

But make no mistake, I'm still in charge, which is why I took their car keys and hid them, so they have to ask permission to go anywhere. I'm starting to get used to this role reversal thing.

Counting the days (just not sure how many).

Denise

Thursday – April 16th, 2020
Dear Diary

When Gina was a toddler, my friend Diane bought her a toy ironing set for her birthday. In front of my mother-in-law, she opened it and asked, *"What's this, Mommy?"* Yeah, I don't know how to iron or sew, for that matter, and I have been so spoiled all these years having Mom do both for me.

I noticed Mom was running out of projects. No more posters to make for her community entertainment committee (which involves a lot of cursing at the computer trying to find where her clip art is hiding). No more sewing to do (which involves a lot of cursing when she can't thread the needles).

So the other day, in an effort to keep Mom busy, I devised a plan called "Operation Iron Clothes." I gave her a pile of my clothes and asked if she wouldn't mind ironing them. Usually, she finds it very therapeutic. But it backfired on me. Dad and her started yelling at each other; he insisted he took the clothes out of the dryer on time and it wasn't necessary for her to iron anything. She told him he didn't take the clothes out in time and that he should mind his own business. It escalated into a full-blown squabble. My plan was ruined. Of course, I probably should have told them that since I haven't been wearing anything other than PJs and bathing suits, I deviously and purposely wrinkled my clean clothes.

I also forgot that when she does iron for me, she always reminds me that I'm almost 62 and "*When are you ever going to learn how to do this yourself?*"

The few times I attempted to iron, she'd yell, "*You don't even have the ironing board positioned the right way; what is wrong with you?*"

I am now using her own famous line against her: "*Leave me alone, I'm [62], I can do what I want.*"

And trust me, learning how to iron is not on my bucket list.

Oh, the best-laid plans.

Now I need a Plan B.

Later,

Denise

Friday – April 17th, 2020
Dear Diary

I'm sure I'm not alone in allowing the small stuff to drive you crazy these days.

And at this point, it's all small stuff. And I am going crazy.

I'm sure others mumble obscenities under their breath when the person before them leaves their coffee pod in the Keurig coffee maker. Am I right? At work (when I had a job in the good old days), it used to drive me crazy when the guys left their pods in the machine with no regard for the person that followed them. And when you think about it, they probably had to dispose of a pod left in the machine before they prepared to make their own cup. So did it ever dawn on them not to do the same? Noooooo.

Just walk away with no consideration for others.

Mom does it every single day. When I wake up, I am completely out of it until I have my first cup of coffee. Because my brain is still asleep, I can't register whether the pod was already used by Mom or I actually put a new one there, and out comes the obscenities.

So I asked Mom, "*Why do you not throw out your coffee pod?*"

She nonchalantly replied, *"I'm usually the only one that drinks coffee, so I'm not used to having to share the machine."*

Followed by, *"What's the big deal?"* *"Get over it."* This from the woman who has obsessive-compulsive tendencies.

Oh Diary, I just re-read this entry and realized that I am losing it and I need to re-read Richard Carlson's book, *Don't Sweat the Small Stuff, and It's All Small Stuff.*

Have no fear; once my coffee kicks in, I'll feel much, much better.

Later,

Denise

Saturday – April 18th, 2020
Dear Diary

We've had a few rainy days now, increasing our desire to binge-watch some television shows and movies.

Now I've already shared the many reasons why I refuse to watch TV with Mom. Unfortunately, Dad isn't much better. He loves to talk and yell at the TV. Mom and I keep thinking he is on the phone or someone is in the condo visiting because he has full-blown conversations, *"How stupid is that?" "Why would you do that?" "What is wrong with you?"* And don't get me started on stunts. *"Look at that, that's not possible."* And so forth and so on.

I feel like I'm with a toddler who thinks the characters on TV are real. I mean, if he wants reality, then he should watch reality tv or sports instead of his lineup of make-believe sitcoms and medical/police/drama shows. And if he thinks the characters' actions are so dumb, he shouldn't bother watching. I just want to scream, *"Chill out, it's not real!"*

Instead, I put on my headphones and watch a wide array of shows on my laptop that allows me to bask in the glory of escaping reality *(and don't forget the cocktails).*

That's entertainment.

Denise

Sunday – April 19th, 2020
Dear Diary

Day 43

I'm really starting to crack.

I miss church. Today as I watched mass on my laptop, I added a few personal prayers:

Dear Lord,

Please give me strength.

Please give me patience.

Please give me coping skills.

Please don't make me earn another thirty-day badge because sixty days will put me over the edge.

Please, oh, please get me out of this condo, this town, and this state.

Amen

I miss my kids, my friends, my neighborhood, my home, my bed, my TV, and most of all, my sanity.

Like the scene from one of my favorite movies, *The Wizard of Oz*, I keep clicking my heels three times, saying, *"There's no place like home."*

I even grabbed a pair of red shoes from Mom's closet (of course, she has them in every color) and clicked away and still no luck.

I am still here!

So on that note, it's time for another martini.

Later,

Denise

Meme of the day: *A Man Walks Into a Bar, Lucky Bastard!*

Monday – April 20th, 2020
Dear Diary

I saw an interesting meme on Facebook:

ME: *I think I'm ready to date again.*

The universe: *Oh yeah?* [releases worldwide virus preventing all human interaction]

ME: *Well played.*

I've always been the single token person in my group of friends. It's never been a problem because they never make me feel like a third wheel. As the years go by, I become more and more content with my well-rounded life surrounded by a supportive family and great friends.

Only once in a blue moon do I consider dipping my feet in the dating pool. I sometimes, but rarely, fantasize about having a plus one for social events or a vacation companion. Even when that happens, I don't make any effort to pursue it like a bucket list goal. Yup, I'm content.

Growing up, Mom and Dad were great role models on the merits of marriage. Yes, they fight, squabble, and drive each other crazy, but this is balanced with a definite feeling that one can't live without the other. Deep down, there is respect. They are two imperfect people who refuse to give up on each other. Sixty-two years of marriage and counting, it's been a lovely thing to witness.

I've been so busy experiencing isolation with my parents that I haven't questioned any of my family members or friends on how their relationships are holding up in this pandemic. My fingers are crossed that they are doing fine and confirming that they can successfully grow old with their chosen partner. I wish them the strength to ride out the ups and downs and make it to 60+ years intact. I offer them this quote: *"True love is spending one day getting married and the rest of your life feeling glad you did."*

For me, despite being surrounded by a happily married couple, I continue to question whether I'll ever share my living space (or remote control) with another human being. At this point, I'm actually excited about the prospect of going home and returning to isolation, only this time by myself.

This much is for sure: When I do return home, you will not see my profile on any dating sites. And if anyone offers to play "matchmaker," I'll politely decline, grab my remote control and enjoy my personal space.

Still happily single,

Denise

Tuesday – April 21st, 2020
Dear Diary

It's bad enough when you are isolated from others in such close quarters. It's even worse when you all decide to start dieting.

Think of the abundance of crankiness in those two scenarios.

Dad is pretty disciplined when he makes up his mind to be 'good' in the food department. He'll drop four pounds in a day and Mom and I will be completely disgusted at the ease with which the weight comes off him.

I have a long way to go, but I'm very satisfied that I have not *gained* any weight since I've been here. It will be a slow, long journey to shed some pounds, and I've challenged myself to make no excuses, walk every day, and cut down on my food (and alcohol) intake.

Mom, well, she just drives you to drink, which of course, does not help the goal of cutting calories. She counts her points using her Weight Watchers chart and records everything except the cheats. She doesn't record when she sneaks a snack or 'tastes' and 'picks' on all the food she is preparing. The best is when she tries to tell us what we should and shouldn't be eating. *Like she's our coach.*

We fight at the dinner table, each of us judging the other's plate. It's enough to make you lose your appetite, which I guess in the long run would help with the dieting.

I've instituted a new rule: Everyone worries about themselves, no commenting on what the other is eating. Pretty soon, we will have to drag out the snack tables, and each eats our meals in a different corner of the condo.

Dieting is painful.

Denise

Wednesday – April 22nd, 2020
Dear Diary

For some strange reason, I want to start calling my mother 'Jenny'.

I don't know why, really, but I thought after all this time together, it would be a fun experiment.

Jeannette (Caruso) Ostuni is 'GiGi' to her great-grandchildren, 'Grandma' to all the grandkids, 'Aunt Jenny' to all my cousins, 'Sis' to her brothers, and 'Jenny' to all her friends. My siblings and I call her 'Mom' or 'Ma' and sometimes 'Mother' when we are trying to get her attention. Believe it or not, I still occasionally call her 'Mommy'; after all, she *is* my mommy. Between my upbringing (instilling that we address all adults with respect), as well as 60 years of habit, it is hopeless, and I just can't seem to call her Jenny.

Mom does what all of us moms do when we are around kids; we mix up their names. I constantly yell, *"Jamie, I mean Andrew, whoever you are,"* and I'm always confusing Angela (my sister) with Gina (my daughter). It's a common practice.

When we have our family gatherings, Mom constantly mixes up Angela and me. No biggie. Except now I think she has a whole new slew of nicknames for me, not to be confused with anyone else.

This is what confinement does to a person because now I'm often referred to as:

- Bi%$#
- Miss Know It All
- Pain in the A@#
- Whatever your name is
- You F*^%$@

I may need that therapy again.

Sincerely,
Denise Grace Rita (Ostuni) Fucito

Thursday – April 23rd, 2020
Dear Diary

Pase, mi casa es su casa. (Come on in, my home is your home.)

When you are living in someone else's home, you have to adapt to their décor and lifestyle.

Mom and Dad dwell in their condo in Florida and their house on Candlewood Lake. In addition, they have a cottage on Johnny's farm. All their homes have common quirks.

I've written several entries about the kitchen, which Mom has now dubbed a "War Zone." We'll just deem the kitchen as a space that is not meant to be shared with others.

Like every home these days, there are chargers scattered about for the cell phones, iPad, Kindles, and hearing aids. All labeled, of course, compliments of Mom. It's very efficient and makes for easy navigation.

There are throw rugs everywhere – every size and style. I'm constantly tripping on one of them. They are in front of the beds, the sides of the beds, the kitchen, the bathrooms, the hallway. It's like living in a giant jigsaw puzzle, and the rugs are the puzzle pieces.

Mom has garbage baskets every ten feet all throughout the condo.

When you help take out the garbage, it feels like you're on an Easter egg hunt when making sure you've emptied all the baskets.

When the phone rings, you find yourself spinning around like an idiot trying to figure out which one to answer. They have seven, yes, seven landline phones (for one phone line) in a 1600 square foot condo. When they ring all at once, you feel like it's a fire drill. I want to flee for my life.

Now, most senior citizens scatter reading glasses throughout their living space. Nothing unusual about that, right? At my parent's homes, rosary beads can also be found in every nook and cranny. They are everywhere, the balcony, the bathrooms, the kitchen, the nightstands, etc. I mean, let's face it, saying your prayers while you're using the bathroom facilities can be pretty convenient if you are a multi-tasker at heart.

Other than that, the homes are comfortable and quaint. And who am I to complain since I'm here as a guest? To each his own.

Denise

Friday – April 24th, 2020
Dear Diary

Mom keeps mumbling; she wants to write a retaliation diary. She printed my entries and swore she could defend all that has been written about her.

This prompted me to give her a lesson on the difference between 'slander' (i.e., what you verbally say about a person) and 'libel' (i.e., what you write about a person). I wanted her to have a correct understanding of these terms before she filed her lawsuit.

My response to her taking such actions was: "*Really*?" followed by:

So you don't fall asleep constantly when watching TV?

You don't have issues when trying to send emails with attachments?

You don't have a bug up your butt about Dad making the bed?

Don't you have a problem with the way we use your precious kitchen?

Don't you leave the coffee pods in the machine?

You don't make sure your shoes match your outfit?

Do you actually know the difference between Facebook and AOL?

Don't you think vagina wipes are an acceptable substitute for Wet Ones?

Finally!

"Mom, I don't mean to pick on you; however, if you were Pinocchio, your nose wouldn't fit in this condo if you think the statements I've made aren't true!"

So now she admits she can't refute what's been written about her, but she can have ball writing stuff about me.

I admit I'm impossible to live with; I'm a royal pain in the butt, I'm impatient, I love to mess up her kitchen, and many other unpleasant things.

And between you and me, it's all part of my diabolical plan (to be continued)

Later,

Denise

Saturday – April 25th, 2020
Dear Diary

A while back, my girlfriends and I had a 'Zoom' Happy Hour, and we posed questions like *"What do you miss most since being in isolation?"* and *"What is the first thing you want to do when you are no longer homebound?"* Finally, *"While in isolation, what have you learned about yourself that you didn't know before?"*

On one of our field trips to the stores, Dad, Mom and I were chatting away about all the things we miss and all the things we want to do when life gets back to normal, or at least the 'new' normal. Mom can't wait to garden, and Dad wants to work around the farm. Me, I cannot wait to hug and squeeze my precious grandson, Tommy.

When I posed the last question to Mom, she immediately replied,

"What have I learned about myself? I know now that I am so glad we have that long-term assisted living insurance policy because there is no way I am ever going to live with any of my children."

I guess I ruined her, and boy do my siblings owe me *big time*.

I am diabolical.

Denise

(Honestly, though, if we survived this isolation together so far, they can cancel the insurance policy).

Sunday – April 26th, 2020
Dear Diary

We had a sibling email last weekend in which my brother Johnny suggested that we start thinking about a departure date *"before someone gets hurt down there."*

They must be so confused when they speak to each of us separately and get three different versions of what life is like here.

I'll let you in on a little secret – I am actually enjoying this bonding experience with my parents; it's on a level like no other. As I stated earlier, I lived at home for twenty-five years and didn't know a fraction of the inner workings of my parents like I have learned in the last 48 days. The scariest part is I have a deeper understanding of what makes me tick based on the traits I have inherited from both of them.

The other day my (Gemini) horoscope said, *"The reason for some of your behaviors can be summed up in four little words: It's in your blood."*

Lucky me. I've got the best and worst of each of them running through my veins. I have Dad's impatience, passion when arguing a viewpoint (which sometimes involves vein-popping), and the incredible need for social interaction. We love a full social calendar. I'd like to think I have Mom's organizational skills and the generous spirit that prompts her to help others (she needs to wear a T-shirt that states, "*Just say no!*").

I've been so intertwined with them that I'm not always sure what traits are my own, those free of their genetic influences. What I have learned is that I spend many hours trying not to adopt the traits in Mom that drive me crazy (which in the long run is for my kids' sakes). Last summer, my friends bought me a dish towel that says, *"Sometimes I open my mouth, and my mother comes out."* But all kidding aside, Jenny is one of a kind, so I won't fight the inevitable too much.

I'm no dummy; I'm fully aware that it's just a matter of time before *my* children start dropping hints about how I should consider purchasing long-term assisted living insurance.

Karma!

Denise

Monday – April 27th, 2020
Dear Diary

And so it has begun. We discussed our departure date (which is planned for Saturday), but Dad and I refuse to confirm the exact day and time with Mom. Unfortunately, this has not prevented her from delving into her neurotic stage of departure packing.

With the exception of the actual car trip home, having to listen to her complain the whole time, this is the part where Dad and I keep shaking our heads at the insanity she will put us through before we leave.

All the items in the pantry are now on one shelf. This goes for the refrigerator too. Dad and I keep sighing because we just don't understand her logic that it takes longer to pack items up if they are on several shelves. Seriously? It's like a brainteaser: How much extra time would it require to pack stuff into a box from one shelf or several if it's the same number of items? Then again, I no longer equate Mom with logic.

She has slowly started sneaking boxes (food, files, clothes, etc.) to the garage for packing as if we can't do that the day before we leave. Nope. Now I purposely ask her for things that I know she already brought down, so she has to keep going to the garage to get them. It's good exercise. She's discreet about it because she doesn't want to admit it's absurd.

When she starts to pile up the boxes, she gets nervous about what might not fit in the van. To avoid battling with Dad, she slyly compiles a box of 'light' items and sneaks to the post office to have it shipped home. (She ships to my house so it can be stored out of sight until she can unpack it without him noticing). This, by the way, is an annual event.

All of this is just another reminder of why I never volunteer to take them home. I'm all in for bringing them down in November, but I'm out for the return trips, after this one, of course.

I just wish I could give her some type of drug that will make her think we have just arrived in Florida instead of her knowing we are leaving. Or at least give me a drug that blocks out my memory of this final week.

Shoot Me Now

Denise

Tuesday – April 28th, 2020
Dear Diary

We've been together so long now that I've decided to start categorizing my parents' "arguments."

Now, don't get me wrong, the marriage is rock solid, and despite all this time together, it is still apparent that one can't live without the other. I'm convinced that this quarantine stuff is going to destroy people who had shaky marriages going in, and I'm confident couples that have been together more than fifty years will likely survive. Only time will tell if this hypothesis proves to be true.

So arguments are now categorized as 'tiffs,' 'spats,' 'squabbles,' 'ongoing battles,' and 'fights' (like the ones you saw in the schoolyard when you shouted 'fight, fight, fight').

I was privy to a little 'tiff' the other day when Mom got upset at Dad when he took it upon himself to instruct her on how to eat a grapefruit. *"Cut it into smaller slices, then take the skin off, so it doesn't squirt all over."* She instead decided to be spiteful and cut it into four quarters (she butchered that poor grapefruit) and then picked at it like it was a bone. As she complained to me about what a pain he is and dubbed him Mr. *"Know it All,"* I replied, *"Hey, no fair, that's one of my nicknames!"* But the irony of this scenario was that a few hours later, she was 'instructing' me on how to fry chicken cutlets, and I just said, *"Really?" "Do you not see the hypocrisy here?"*

She did not.

My favorite argument is the 'ongoing battle' that has to do with magazines. All couples argue about money, but my parents are generally in sync when it comes to their spending habits.

A little background: Dad has always been a big proponent of 'work hard' and "play hard," and he was successful in achieving work-life balance. Growing up, we had many luxuries and toys (e.g., built-in pool, camping trailer, snowmobiles, jet skis, etc.) He'd write a check, no questions ask, for anyone that needed money. This generosity has always been balanced with some thriftiness, like turning the catsup bottle over to make sure every drop is used or turning off the hot water when we were in the shower too long. And OMG, if you left the refrigerator door opened too long, you got his wrath.

I grocery shop with them a lot. Every time we shop together, Mom sneaks a magazine on the conveyor belt, which then becomes "the battle." He thinks they are overpriced and filled with nothing but ads. She replies, *"Who cares? You spend a fortune on your stupid motorcycle trips, so I'll buy the damn magazine."* Every single time, it's the same exchange.

There are many solutions, such as Mom should buy the magazines when she shops alone because he isn't one to hover over receipts. Another simpler solution is that my siblings and I should just get her magazine subscriptions as a Mother's Day gift.

Meanwhile, there are magazines strewn all over the condo next to the rosary beads.

So it's all good,

Denise

Wednesday – April 29th, 2020
Dear Diary

Mom and I share a Kindle account. We love our paperwhite Kindles because when experiencing bouts of insomnia, we can just flip it open and read away.

The beauty of sharing an account is that we can purchase books that can be downloaded on both our devices (two for the price of one). We often have mini book clubs about what we each thought of a book we read and then discuss which one we should tackle next.

The funny thing is that Mom reads her books the same way she watches television. She falls asleep and then has to re-read the chapter and figure out what's going on in the story. It probably takes about ten tries to get through a chapter (just like her recorded TV shows). Then she'll start asking me questions about the characters, and I can't remember them because I've already read four other books since she started the first one.

Another downside is the technical difficulties. I am absolutely horrible when it comes to assisting her on the computer. I just become downright nasty when she starts with the *"I don't know what's wrong with my Kindle." "I lost my place in the book." "Why did the font change?"*

"Can you help me figure out if I read this one already?" OMG, she's killing me.

Lately, there have been fewer technical difficulties, and today marks a whole week without her asking me a single question about her Kindle. Progress.

When we do finally arrive home, I will have to continue to play the 'help' desk for her since my services include a lifetime warranty.

Still learning to be patient,

Denise

Thursday – April 30th, 2020
Dear Diary

When I was younger, I dubbed Mom *"The Mileage Queen."* For some strange reason, she was (and still is) obsessed with knowing how many miles it is from Point A to Point B. *"It's 10.8 miles to the mall." "It's 4.2 miles from the house to church."* I'm not quite sure how the importance of this information fits into the grand scheme of life, but it apparently matters a great deal to her.

We are gearing up for our departure from Florida back to Connecticut on Saturday. Years ago, I noticed in their glove compartment that she keeps a record (mileage and time) of their trips to and from Florida. I'm thinking I should go sneak a peek so I can brace myself for whatever world's record we are going to have to try and break on this trip!

Now many of you have heard me tell the tales of our trips down to Florida in November. We drive straight through (19–20 hours). Mom's famous quote when she gets in the car and before Dad even starts the engine is *"Never again."* After all this isolation, she seems to be ready and willing to embrace our trip home. I'm positive that her enthusiasm will dissipate within the first hour we are in the car.

Instead of a swear jar, I'm going to make her put $1 in the jar every time she says any variation of 'Never again' or 'This is the last time I'm driving in this car to or from Florida'. I'm pretty sure by the end of the trip; I'll be rich enough that I won't even need to claim my unemployment benefits for the week!

Wish us luck,
Denise

P.S. Dad has decided to make this trip a little more challenging. Yesterday he pulled a hamstring on his left leg, so I'll be doing most of the closing up condo tasks, packing the car, and driving. Everyone says, stay another week. Nope. Not happening; we are out of here.

Friday – May 1st, 2020
Dear Diary

This is it. We are leaving sometime in the early morning tomorrow, thus ending our adventure of 55 days.

The circle of life is an amazing journey.

When you are a child, you view your parents as these authoritarian, disciplinary drill sergeants. You don't view them as friends. Then you spend your teenage years complaining about them and thinking of them as out-of-touch "fuddy-duddies." Then you grow up and come to appreciate them when you are raising your own family. Everything begins to flip as your kids begin to view you the same way. And so forth and so on.

I've always believed that the most important things you can pass on to your children are traditions and memories. When all is said and done, none of the material things matter, and I mean none. You will look back and just remember holidays, vacations, parties, traditions, and most of all, memories. A quote from the character Carson in Downton Abbey: *"The business of life is the acquisition of memories."*

For me, some examples include the Caruso cousins flying kites at the Elwood farm on Palm Sunday. The

Ostuni/Cavanagh Thanksgiving at the Big House with Aunt Anna cooking thirty-five variations of vegetables. Pool parties on Solow Lane with a revolving door of relatives and neighbors. And my strangest childhood memory was at Easter time when Mom and Dad made us sit around our dining room table doing the rosary every night during Lent. She had these bionic rosary beads that took up the whole table. Angela would sit properly and take it all seriously while Johnny, Charlie and I sat sideways in our seats, ready to make a mad dash for the door as soon as the last Hail Mary was recited.

I never thought I would make so many new memories with my parents at this stage in my life. I know my kids will make fun of me (actually, they already do), and I'll know it is out of love, just as my teasing of my parents has been out of love.

And now it's time to brace my siblings.

It's their turn.

No cheating; they can't alternate.

Each will be sentenced to thirty consecutive days in their homes with Mom and Dad as their house guests.

They will get to experience all the joy (and pain) I have.

Johnny, Charlie, and Angela get ready for the ride of your life.

Here are some reminders and tips:

- You will lose you hearing from the TV blasting
- You will fear for your life when Dad drives you anywhere
- You will not be allowed to use all your countertop space in the kitchen

- You will run in circles trying to slow Dad down and speed Mom up
- You will feel like a professional mediator or an umpire or a referee
- You will have to dispose of Mom's coffee pods in your coffee maker
- You will do a lot (and I mean a lot) of repeating yourself (tip: make sure the hearing aids are actually in their ears before talking)
- You will feel like an IT 'help desk' operator
- You will say the words 'shoot me now' all day long
- And finally, you will appreciate every single minute of it as I have

Good luck! We'll be home soon.

I've already made shell badges marked "30" for you.

So, who is first, and where do I drop them off?

Denise

PS: You may occasionally receive future entries.

Welcome Back to Connecticut

The Sequel – Living Next Door
Sunday – May 3rd, 2020
Dear Diary

The journey home was yet another adventure, of course. We managed to beat our record and make it safely back to Connecticut in 16.5 hours.

Dad woke me up at 1:30 am for our departure. While I was getting ready, I overhead Mom saying to him, "*Tough, I'm not waiting to get in the car. I'm saying it now, 'never again'*". She pretty much made those types of comments every half hour throughout the entire trip.

We left the parking lot at exactly 2:09 am. I know this because Mom was recording every aspect of the trip in her journal. We were in Georgia within three and a half hours. This was possible because there was no one on the road, and Dad drove really fast.

I took over the driving at our first gas refill stop, which Mom recorded to be at 6:29 am. Even though I only drove for four hours of the entire trip, I managed to be the one that got pulled over by a police officer in South Carolina. It wasn't for speeding, but apparently, I was supposed to move into the middle lane when he was pulled over with another car. As he was approaching the van, Mom said to me, *"I better put my phone down, or we'll get in trouble."* Of course, I was cracking up because she wasn't driving, and I'm pretty sure it's OK to look at your phone when you're a passenger. The officer was not happy and took my license and registration with every intention of giving me a ticket (which he informed me carries a $1,000 fine). I just think when he saw the car packed with Dad lying in the back and Mom in the front looking all confused, he actually read my thought bubble, which was screaming, *"Please just let me get home! I can't take another minute of this."* Sure enough, he read my mind and, with sympathy, said, *"Are you heading back to Connecticut? I'm just going to give you a warning, get home safe."* Whew.

We made three gas refill stops, two of which included a drive-through McDonald's run. When we grabbed our Egg McMuffins for breakfast, Dad wanted me to pull right into the gas station before we even ate them. I threw a hissy fit and begged him not to make us multi-task breakfast with filling up the gas tank. I just wanted to stretch outside the car and breathe. It was bad enough I felt like I was being demoted from confinement in the condo to the back seat of a mini-van. I needed some space.

During the middle of the trip, I decided to watch a movie that was downloaded on my phone. As I put on my headphones and hit play, I didn't make it past the opening credits when Mom started asking about her iPhone. *"How do I send the text?"* *"Where are my contacts?"* OMG, I went from the computer to the Kindle, and now I had to give iPhone lessons. I'll admit I was a little snippy. Thank goodness there were rosary beads in the car, so I was able to say a lot of prayers as we soared through the states to our final destination.

We are all unpacked and slowly getting into our old routine as next-door neighbors. We went to my daughter's house for dinner, and Mom wore her beautiful red pants set with matching shoes and earrings. Me, I'm still adjusting to having to pick out outfits to wear (and trying not to forget to include a bra with my selections).

Life is good.

Denise

Wednesday – May 13th, 2020
Dear Diary

Well, it's been about a week and a half since we returned from Florida. The weather is so inconsistent, including some snow on May 9th. I went from long walks on the beach in a bathing suit to walks around our community in sweatshirts and sometimes a winter coat. What were we thinking coming home to such crappy weather?

There are not too many regrets, though. Spending Mother's Day with my kids, having full control of the remote control, and working on house projects have more than made up for the weather. I kept hearing how everyone was cleaning closets and drawers and catching up on neglected projects, and I wasn't able to take advantage of that while in Florida.

So, I am the master of my domain once again. Yet, with Mom and Dad next door, I'm still faced with some babysitting challenges. The good news is that they are constantly busy. Setting up the house for the summer, gardening (oh how they love to spread mulch), and visiting the farm are keeping them active like two Energizer Bunnies. They truly run circles around me.

Here are some things that haven't changed:

*I still play IT help desk kindle, phone, and computer. As soon as I walk through the door, they present me with one dilemma or another.

*I still have to search the desk for clues as to where they've gone when the car is missing. Doctor appointment? Farm? Stores? I need to set up some type of video surveillance, so I can see when they leave the driveway. They still leave their phones behind, so a location tracker would be useless.

*They still argue over the stupidest things. My brother spent two days with them at the farm and commented about how annoying their arguments are, and I just cracked up. Wait, dear brother, try 30 days in a row. I did my time.

Here are some things that have changed:

*Mom seems to be enjoying the kitchen at the lake house so much better than the Florida condo. It's big, and it's all hers. She can enjoy her designated counter space without me splashing water on her precious countertop.

*Dad is so much busier here with constant projects. I don't have to purposely break the vacuum cleaner to give him something to do. He had issues with his hot tub, major plumbing challenges setting up my outdoor shower, routine tasks getting the golf carts ready, and tons of mini fixer-upper things to work on, all in just one week. Give that man a hammer and a screwdriver, and he is as happy as can be, and he really should have his own HGTV DIY show.

*They are back to their old routine of making the bed every day. I still haven't wrapped my head around that debacle in Florida.

*Of course, the biggest change is that I am no longer in their space. Last spring, I had bats in my house, and I had to move into their guest room for a week until the situation was resolved. I was still working in the city and had access to my house during the day, so it does not compare to almost two months in the Florida condo. I love, love, love my home, kitchen, bed, patio, and remote control.

Sitting here on my laptop at a desk in the kitchen, I am most grateful for the view. It includes the lake and my parents' house. I am going to enjoy the summer watching Mom and Dad buzz around on their golf carts, Dad checking to see if I need anything to be fixed, and Mom walking up the slight hill to my house to borrow something or drop off items or just visit.

The road that separates our houses is like a moat around a castle.

It gives me just the right amount of space to feel free to do all the things I couldn't do while hanging in the Florida condo.

There really is no place like home.

Later,

Denise (a/k/a Dorothy from the Wizard of Oz)

Monday – June 1ˢᵗ, 2020
Dear Diary

We've been home now for a month. Home is still great. And with Mom and Dad next door, some things have changed, and some have not.

Today it's my birthday, and I have been reflecting on all the blessings bestowed upon me. As Mom came over to wish me a happy birthday, I decided to pick her brain about my humble beginnings. This is what she remembers:

Mom and Dad were only 21 when they had me, which was exactly nine months after the honeymoon. (They had to prove to Blue Cross/Blue Shield that they were indeed married.) It was such a different and simpler time. Mom craved watermelon during her pregnancy, and back then, you couldn't just go to a store and buy a watermelon. Grandpa made a trip to the NYC Farmer's Market to satisfy her cravings. When she went into labor, Dad dropped her off at the hospital and didn't return until the 2ⁿᵈ day (apparently, he was working three jobs back then). When he did finally get to the hospital, he started to feel faint (the man used to drop like a hammer at the sight of a needle), and Mom had to remind him that she was the one who had the baby and he needed to get past his phobias. They had agreed on the name Grace but then changed their mind because there were so many family members with that name. She still regrets that decision. Denise was just a name she liked as a second choice, and Dad joked, later on, they should have named me June because of my June 1st arrival (I'm glad that was only a joke). They lived in their first home on Solow Lane, and when Mom came home with me from the hospital, Grandpa Ostuni had a bouquet of flowers in a Madonna (religious, not the pop singer) vase in the nursery. She said Dad was a hands-on father; even though he was always working, he did change diapers, feed me, etc. She loved to dress me up in different outfits and take pictures with a pegboard in the background spelling out some kind of related statement (the label maker wasn't invented yet). Even though Mom had a good job as a secretary before they were married, she couldn't wait to be a stay-at-home mom. She never returned to work until Dad started the business eight years later. She always told me that if anyone asked her what she wanted to be when she grew up, she would answer *"a wife and a mother."* I guess my birth helped her fulfill that wish.

So as I finish eating a piece of birthday cake, washed down with a slice of watermelon, I am taking a moment to thank Mom and Dad for giving me life, raising me, being role models, and entertaining me on a daily basis. I am grateful to begin my 62nd year with neighbors like them!

But you should hear what my neighbor did the other day. *To be continued…*

Denise

Tuesday – June 2nd, 2020
Dear Diary

My neighbor, a/k/a Mom, wandered over to my house the other morning, asking for help in scanning a document. I walked her through it and typed up instructions on how to retrieve the scan and send it to the recipient. She murmured, *"OK, but if I can't figure it out, you can just come over and show me again."*

I simply can't hide from this help desk role that has followed me from Florida to Connecticut.

There are some benefits, though, because while she was at my house, she got roped into helping me replace the shelf liner. She even took it a step further and started cleaning the shelves for me.

So moving forward, I've decided not to make any house calls; it's drop-off services only. Next time she comes over, I'll start refolding the towels in my linen closet. She is sooooo good at that (and sheets too). She's always yelling at me to learn how to do it right. Now I can respond, *"It's OK if I can't remember; you can always come over and show me again."*

It's like a battle between an IT Help Desk Operator and a Domestic Engineer (Susie Homemaker).

That Susie is so spunky.

Denise

Wednesday – June 3rd, 2020
Dear Diary

Mom has been a gardening machine since we returned home. She's made multiple trips to multiple nurseries gathering zillions of bushes and flowers to plant. It is amazing how happy she is when covered in dirt. In addition, she enjoys researching various flowers and making recommendations for landscape ideas for anyone who asks (sort of like a gardening 'help desk'). Aside from all the gardening, she is constantly making floral arrangements with any flowers she can find.

This is not a passion we share. She often tells people that she can't understand how her genes were not passed on to me. About 30 years ago, she assisted me when I attempted to plant tulips at our home in Kings Park. Unfortunately, I put the whole row of bulbs upside down, and she had to replant everything. I declared later that day that I will never have an interest in anything garden-related, and from that point on, I surrendered all my homes to her for outdoor decorating.

I kind of wish I didn't feel that way. The other day Mom was talking to my friend Cathy about flowers and plants, blah, blah, blah, and when I came over to them, they actually 'shooshed' me. They gave me a look like, "*you have no interest in any of this, so be on your way.*" A part of me was a little jealous, but still not enough to take up gardening.

So I will continue to embrace sharing my mother and her gardening expertise. After all, she still needs me to help her with editing (anything she writes she requests I proofread/edit) and technology needs (kindle, phone, computer, printer/scanner). Mom remains the gardening expert and a domestic goddess, while I remain the teacher for all things non-gardening, and together we help each other survive day-today.

However, when it comes to cooking, it's almost a tie, and so the kitchen battles continue.

Denise

Thursday – June 4th, 2020
Dear Diary

A few weeks ago, Mom and I were preparing for a family gathering and decided to make homemade Mac n Cheese. This time she came to my house/my kitchen. Unlike her Florida kitchen with the designated 12 inch square counter space, we spread out and made a complete mess. There was elbow macaroni on the floor, and every inch of counter space was utilized. When she began mixing the sauce with the pasta, she was overzealous and starting mushing it, which led me to yell that she was ruining the batch. It was like having a reverse flashback to our kitchen spats in Florida.

The real lesson of this scenario is about appreciating the amount of control you have when you are in your own space. I was reminded of the fact that I was merely a guest in their home regardless of how overstayed my visit was, and now I am now home sweet home and get to enjoy food preparation on my terms. We truly are masters of our domain.

And our cooking battles continue.

This last month Mom has been struggling with her cooking skills by leaving out ingredients. She doesn't realize how many times she has asked me to remind her how to cook something. It's not just an age thing; I think some of it can be attributed to her lack of passion for cooking these days (she yearns to garden 24/7). If I casually invite her to dinner, she immediately jumps on it, "*Yes, we'll be over; what time?*" Gone are the days I had to coax her into joining me for dinner.

I think I win the Golden Spatula Award for surpassing her cooking skills. However, it's all good since we barter my *'meals on wheels' for her 'landscape services'.*

Now it's time to pass the cooking torch onto my daughter, Gina, so I can secure my own future of dinner invites. Don't get me wrong; she is not a bad cook (although her brothers are better at it); it's just that she isn't motivated to take her cooking skills up a notch. So I'll have to start with sparking her interest in the kitchen, then move on to actual lessons.

I'm determined to have three generations of golden spatula award winners.

Later,

Denise

Monday – June 15th, 2020
Dear Diary

A few days ago, Mom called me to the computer to show me a picture she printed of Suzie Orman. She announced she wants to send it to her hairdresser because she wants to style her hair the same way.

This led to three spats.

The first one being me making a snippy comment, *"I hope you don't think she can make you look like her."* Boy, did she bite my head off, *"Of course not, I'm not stupid, I just want that type of hairstyle."* OK, I was trying to be funny in a sarcastic way.

Strike one for me. (My sarcasm fell flat)

The second fight was trying to find the photo online again. She printed it but couldn't remember what site she got it from. When I tried to grab the mouse to check the browser, she smacked my hand and said, *"I'm not stupid, I'll find it."* I left the room.

Strike two for me. (Geez, I was just trying to help)

The third fight wasn't really a fight. It would have involved me attempting to show her how to save a copy and email it, this would involve way too much time and patience to explain how to do this, so I just walked away and told her to figure it out herself. She gave up after five minutes.

Strike three for me. (OK, I abandoned her)

I needed to make up for my three strikes. When she wasn't looking, I took a picture of the picture with my phone. When she met with her hairdresser, I simply opened my phone and displayed a copy instantly.

Mom is still scratching her head, trying to figure out how I was able to produce the photo on my phone. I was only trying to redeem myself. Regardless, her wish was granted and her hair was styled like the picture.

Denise

P.S A month later, she was frustrated with the new style and went back to her old hairdo.

Friday – July 10th, 2020
Dear Diary

125 days

Here's an update on my adventures of living next door to Mom and Dad more than two months since we've returned home. They have had numerous doctors' appointments, and it was discovered that Mom has ear wax build-up, and this has caused a huge reduction in her hearing ability. So between Dad's hearing aids and Mom's wax build-up, I sarcastically suggested they begin to read lips. Either way, I am sure to stand directly in front of them when I am speaking to them.

Dad had to put drops in Mom's ears each night for a week, and he was so unsympathetic, I caught him telling her to keep her head down on the table for the rest of the day. My sister and I will need to be on hand when Mom has her knee (meniscus) surgery next week. I'm pretty sure Dad will not make an adequate nurse.

Dad went on his weeklong motorcycle trip and my sister and I 'babysat' Mom. Basically, we made sure she took it easy, didn't go shopping without telling us where she was going and didn't indulge in eating ice cream for dinner every night, a piece of cake.

We survived the July 4th weekend with the entire immediate family of thirty, and it was great. This holiday is the equivalent of Christmas as far as all family members are expected to be at the lake for the weekend. (It was once said that you are out of the will if you blow it off.) The preparation for the weekend involves a lot of shopping and a lot of cooking. Mom is famous for over-preparation. She tends to prepare meals way too far in advance, and it drives Dad, me, and my sister crazy. At one point, we all ganged up on her and yelled, *"Do not even think of making egg salad three days before you are serving it."* Her response: *"I'm not adding the mayonnaise yet, so what's the big deal?"* This is an ongoing battle. She views it as efficient; we view it as poisonous.

So basically, we are back to our normal family dynamics.

Later,

Denise

Friday – July 17th, 2020
Dear Diary

Mom's meniscus knee surgery was yesterday.

The night before the procedure, she hobbled to my house and said to me, *"We have a problem."* She explained how upset she was because she cannot use the crutches. After practicing for quite a while, she said she felt like she was going to fall. Then she nonchalantly adds to the conversation, *"Oh, by the way, I'm trying to print a recipe, and my printer keeps printing 36 pages over and over again."* I knew there had to be more to the story than her inability to use the crutches. So I once again played help desk and went to fix the printer. I later told my sister that if we ever have to hire caregivers for Mom and Dad, we will need to make sure the candidates have extensive IT skills on their resumes.

The next day, the procedure went very smoothly. But of course, Mom being Mom, she refused to take it easy. She kept getting up and walking with her cane and wouldn't let anyone help her or get the things she needed. She basically acted as if she never had the procedure. My sister became very frustrated and said she couldn't take it anymore. I just laughed and said, *"55 days I dealt with this, suck it up sis."*

The next morning I stopped by to check in on my parents, as well as my sister. Sis informed me Mom was enjoying her pain meds. She said that she did hear moaning in the middle of the night, but it was Dad (in excruciating pain from a pinched nerve), not Mom doing the moaning. Then she reports that Dad missed his 7:30 am therapy appointment this morning, and when the doctor called to tell him he missed the appointment, Dad proceeded to tell the doctor that he had a '*rough night*' and was '*up all night with his wife*'. Mom hears this and perks up and screams, "*Tell him I had surgery. Do you even hear yourself?*"

So basically, things are back to normal.

Later,

Denise

Friday – July 31st, 2020
Dear Diary

Five months have gone by since my adventure began.

Despite the skimpy social calendar this summer, it's been pretty good so far. On the lake, we still get to enjoy boating and the beach, and we have been mini-entertaining with family and friends.

Mom has recovered very nicely from her knee surgery. The other day my daughter said, "*Mom, this will probably upset you, but Grandma is in your garden weeding. She's not on her knees, but she's bending over with her butt in the air.*" I didn't waste my time reprimanding her. Even her physical therapist told her she was uncooperative and difficult, and of course, Mom responded with her usual, "*I'm 83, and you are not going to change me at this point; I can do whatever I want.*"

So the new normal since the pandemic has led to divided families, communities, towns, states, and countries, and I can only say that Mom and Dad have adjusted just fine. They refuse to live in fear. They embrace family and friends without a care in the world. They live life to the fullest every single day, and I can't wait to celebrate their

63rd wedding anniversary on August 31st and their 84th birthdays in September.

As the country continues to go a little crazy this summer of 2020, I remain forever grateful that I get to share this adventure with Mom and Dad.

I'm going to take a break now and sit back and enjoy the remainder of the summer best I can.

Denise

Postscript
Wednesday – October 1st, 2020
Dear Diary

Well, we survived the summer of 2020. Things are still a little hectic as far as restrictions and returning to normal.

Last week my siblings and I had a lovely celebration for our parents' 84th birthday. We shared an intimate lobster bake dinner at my brother Charlie's house. Somehow the eight of us managed to eat four hundred steamed clams followed by lobster, potatoes, corn, and cake. Aside from our appreciation for our parents' good health and well-being, we were grateful for our cholesterol medicine after the butter overload.

At one point during our dinner, we had a very passionate and animated discussion about politics. After about half an hour, Mom stood up and simply stated, *"Enough talks about politics, let's talk about sex."* Well, that shut us up instantly. She continues to speak her mind.

Our next discussion was about the return trip to Florida. For the last 12 years, it has been a tradition that I drive with them to Florida in November. Dad and I share the driving and make the trip with minimal stops in 19–20 hours. It was concluded that I am suffering from PTSD caused by our 16 ½ hour return trip in May. In addition to my daughter expecting my second grandchild in a few weeks, I was glad that my sister insisted she makes the trip with them this time. After all of us ganging up on Dad, we convinced him to stop his marathon mentality and make this trip more leisurely with a tourist stop in Savannah, Georgia. So you can teach an old dog new tricks. However, I have to admit I'm a little jealous that my sister gets to enjoy this journey without the pressure of beating the overall trip time record. And yet, I think my dad is actually a little disappointed I'm not on board for the 'let's beat our record' this time. This is despite his secret disappointment that I shaved off 15 minutes of our 16.5-hour record when I was pulled over on the highway in South Carolina.

Since this adventure began, Mom and Dad turned 84, celebrated their 63rd anniversary, became a great grandparent for the fourth time, rejoiced in another grandchild becoming engaged to be married in September 2021, and continued to not miss a beat in their snowbird life.

Life really is good.

Denise